THE
POWER
of
YOUR
STORY

CONVERSATION GUIDE

BEN ARMENT

THOMAS NELSON
Since 1798

NASHVILLE   DALLAS   MEXICO CITY   RIO DE JANEIRO

Published in Nashville, Tennessee, by Thomas Nelson. Thomas Nelson is a registered trademark of Thomas Nelson, Inc.

Published in association with Yates & Yates, www.yates2.com.

Thomas Nelson, Inc., titles may be purchased in bulk for educational, business, fund-raising, or sales promotional use. For information, please e-mail SpecialMarkets@ThomasNelson.com.

ISBN: 978-1-4016-7725-1

Printed in the United States of America

12 13 14 15 16 QG 1 2 3 4 5 6

CONTENTS

THE POWER OF YOUR STORY
CONVERSATION GUIDE

Welcome to *The Power of Your Story* Conversation Guide. This study is designed to explore the Christian life through the lens of story. Each of the seven sessions is oriented around a classic element in screenwriting. If you enjoy watching movies, you'll love considering your own life through the same storytelling principles. By engaging the biblical narrative, joining the conversations on DVD, and interacting with your study group, you will discover how your story, the biblical story, and God's story all come together in one beautiful masterpiece.

The Power of Your Story experience includes small group discussion. A small group is an excellent place to process the content of the video, ask questions, and learn from others as you listen to what God is doing in their lives. If you are new to small groups, they can be deeply rewarding times of connection and friendship. However, they can also become a disaster if you're not careful. By keeping a few ground rules in mind, you can make your group experience a fruitful one for everyone involved.

First, work to make the group a "safe place." This means being honest about what you're thinking and feeling, as well as listening carefully to everyone else. Second, resist the temptation to "fix" people's problems. Finally, commit to keep everything your group shares confidential. This will foster a rewarding sense of community and give God's Spirit a powerful forum in which to heal, challenge, and transform your lives.

The Power of Your Story experience has the potential to change your life if you let it. Be honest about where you're struggling and resist the temptation to shut down if the content hits too close to home. Examining your life is not an invitation to feel shame, but to open your heart so God's love can flood in. Jesus wants to fill us with his love, and if we seek him with our whole hearts, this is exactly what he will do.

HOW TO USE THIS GUIDE

During each session, you will watch a video where Ben Arment, Ginny Owens, Leonard Sweet, Chris Seay, and Pete Wilson have a conversation related to the highlighted storytelling element. This will be followed by a time of small group discussion. There are plenty of questions for you to use during this time, but you don't have to go through all of them. Your group leader will focus on the ones that are right for you.

Also, your group will be invited to attempt an "Experiments in Story" every week. These are practical exercises meant to personalize and expand the principles you take away from the video. As you reflect on these lessons, you'll be challenged to grow in the practice of your faith. Keep a dedicated notebook or journal with you so you can jot down your thoughts as you attempt each experiment. Starting in Session 2, there will be time before the DVD to report about the previous week's "experiment." This will be a great time to listen to each other and learn from your experiences. Don't worry if you forgot to do the experiment or are just joining the study. Hearing what others have learned is nourishment enough.

Lastly, each session includes daily Bible readings and reflection questions called "Exploring the Story Further." These are opportunities for you to explore the themes from the session by engaging the Bible. Do as many or as few as you like. They are tools to help you, nothing more and nothing less.

Be blessed as you begin your journey through *The Power of Your Story* and know that no matter where you have been or what you have done, God can write your story into a great story.

BACKSTORY

INTRODUCTION

In every great story, there is a moment when we learn the main character's past and understand how it motivates him or her. This revelation is called the backstory. A backstory is often disclosed through action in the plot, and its purpose is to deepen the story at hand. As we discover a character's history, all the bits and pieces of the story we have already seen come into sharper focus and take on new significance. By understanding the past, we can better see the present and the future.

Everyone has a backstory. Our families of origin, past experiences, and successes and failures all dramatically affect the way we see the world. They color the way we feel about ourselves and even influence the way we see God. This makes it complicated when our backstories are filled with pain.

God wants to bring new life out of every place of pain in our lives, but we have to work with him in that process. This work can begin when we take a fearless look at our own backstories. We must acknowledge the things we have done and that we have left undone. Then we must face the pain and regrets we carry and consider whether we are willing to trade them for the good God has for us. Are you willing to trust God with your backstory this week?

STUDYING THE STORY
THE LIFE OF DAVID, PART 1

1 Samuel 16:1–13 details the time when Samuel anointed David as the new king of Israel. Samuel was God's prophet and therefore had the authority to carry out this anointing on behalf of Yahweh. Read the passage out loud and invite the group to consider the following questions:

1. As a group, summarize the story in your own words.

2. Is there anything in the text to indicate that David was an unexpected choice for the new king?

3. Are there any details of the story that seem curious to you and make you wonder if there is a backstory to them?

Now read **1 Samuel 8:1–21** out loud as a group. Discuss the following:

1. Why did the leaders of Israel want a king?

2. Was that a good or bad thing in God's eyes? What did God say the king would do?

3. Reread the 1 Samuel 16 story. What nuances are revealed now that you know some of the backstory?

WATCH THE DVD

Watch *Session #1: Backstory*. When the DVD ends, give members of the group a moment to reflect and jot down one or two things that they learned, disagreed with, or found surprising.

GROUP DISCUSSION

First Impressions

Before everyone shares in the large group, turn to one or two people next to you and finish this sentence, "After watching the video about Backstory one question I have is . . ."

Community Reflections

1. Go around the group and have everyone share their name and one story (from any medium—novel, TV, film, stage play, etc.) that they love to hear over and over.

2. As a group, summarize the video's concept of backstory in your own words.

3. How can your backstory be a blessing? How can it be a curse? What do you think makes that difference?

4. Do you think there is a purpose to everything that happens in our lives? Why or why not?

5. Is it easy or difficult to recognize the ways that your backstory affects how you see yourself? Explain your answer.

6. Do you think it's true that your backstory affects how you see God? Do you recognize any of the ways this is or is not true in your life and faith?

7. Pete says that when it comes to the hurt in your backstory, "If you don't . . . find a place to transform (your) pain, you are just going to transfer (your) pain." What do you think he means? Do you agree? If so, where have you seen examples of this?

8. Who knows your backstory? Are there any parts of your backstory that are difficult to be honest about? Are there any parts that you are trying to hide from yourself, others, or God?

9. What connections to do you find between your backstory and David's backstory? Have you ever heard God call you to serve

him in the middle of a complicated situation? What does God's selection of the smallest and youngest of Jesse's sons say about what God values? Does that sound like good news or bad news to you?

10. Have you ever been like the people of Israel and chased after something everyone else had, even though you were warned it was going to be bad for you?

EXPERIMENTS IN STORY

The backstories of characters in a narrative reveal where people come from and what motivates them. This week, watch a movie, TV show (a pilot works best), read a short story, see a play, or listen to a song (like Johnny Cash's "A Boy Named Sue") and pay attention to how the storyteller employs backstory. Note how the backstory affects the unfolding narrative and what truths it reveals about the characters.

What could you learn from this about how to tell your own story? Make a note of these things in your journal to share next week.

EXPLORING THE STORY FURTHER

This week we have been talking about the way our past sheds light on our present. The language we have used to describe this reality is "backstory." A backstory is what good storytellers include in their narrative so that the audience can understand and relate to the characters. As we have seen from our study of 1 Samuel, characters like David are deeply affected by what has come before, but what about the Bible's main character, God? What can we learn about God by digging deeper into the backstory of the Bible? This week, we will reflect on that question.

Day 1

GENESIS 1:1-2

In the beginning, God created *everything*: the heavens *above* and the earth *below. Here's what happened: At first* the earth lacked shape and was totally empty, and a dark *fog* draped over the deep while God's spirit-wind hovered over the surface of the *empty* waters.

(*Read Genesis 1:3–30 as well)

GENESIS 1:31

Then God surveyed everything He had made, savoring *its beauty and appreciating* its goodness. Evening gave way to morning. That was day six.

Read the scripture for today and consider:

⊞ What is a common theme you find in each act of the creation story?

⊞ What does it say about the God who created all things?

In the beginning, when God created the heavens and the earth, everything was good. The air, water, land, plants, animals, and people were all created perfectly. This is the design and dream of God. This goodness is the way God wants things to be. It is reality when it is right-side-up.

In our reality, we see a world that is broken and upside down. We see the effects of the fall as told in Genesis 3. It is important to remember that the creation story doesn't start there. Our story does not begin with sin; it begins with goodness, and this impacts how we tell God's story. It can also make a difference in how we tell our own stories. Genesis 1 asks us to consider where we think God's story and our stories actually begin. Does the story begin with blessing or curses? The answer to that question may affect more than we realize.

◉ Do you think beginning God's story in Genesis 1 (with good-ness) instead of Genesis 3 (with sin) impacts the way we see God?

◉ Does it affect how we see what God is doing in the world?

◉ When you think about your own story, do you start it with a Genesis 1 orientation or a Genesis 3 orientation? How does your answer to that question influence how you see God, your-self, and the world?

◉ Day 2

DEUTERONOMY 7:6-7

Moses: Remember: you're a people set apart for the Eternal your God; He is your God and has chosen you to be *His own possession*— His special people—out of all the peoples on the earth. The Eternal didn't become devoted to you and choose you because you were the most numerous of all the peoples—in fact, you were the least!

Read the scripture for today and consider:

◈ Why did God choose Israel to be his people?

◈ Why would this matter to God?

When good fortune falls on religious people in our culture, they sometimes say, "God has blessed me." This can make it seem like the evidence of God's favor can be found in our success. It can lead us to believe that the "haves" in this world are somehow more special to God than the "have nots."

The passage in Deuteronomy reveals that this idea is often the reverse of how God actually works. In verse 7, God tells the people that he picked them because they were small. He picked them not in spite of their insignificance, but because of it. He did this in order to show the world his power. When Israel came into the land of promise, there was no doubt that God had been the one leading them, because they were too weak and small to do it themselves.

◈ Do you see God's "blessing" as being the same thing as having strength, resources, and success?

✸ What does Deuteronomy 7:6–7 say about those chosen to work with God?

✸ How can your weaknesses be an opportunity to show God's strength?

 Day 3

MARK 1:1-4

This is the beginning of the good news of Jesus, the Anointed One, *the Liberating King,* the Son of God.

Isaiah the prophet told us *what would happen before He came:*

Watch, I will send My messenger in front of You
    to prepare Your way and make it clear *and straight.*
You'll hear him, a voice crying in the wilderness,
    "Prepare the way of the Eternal One,
    a straight way in the wandering desert, a highway for our
        God."

That messenger was John the Baptist, who appeared in the desert *near the Jordan River* preaching that people should be ritually cleansed through baptism *with water as a sign of* both their changed hearts and God's forgiveness of their sins.

Read the scripture for today and consider:

▨ Why do you think the account of Jesus' life begins with a story about someone else?

Mark begins his gospel about Jesus with stories of John the Baptist because even Jesus has a backstory. Through John, God was fulfilling promises and assurances that had been made generations before. God's story would reach its climax with Jesus, but those who wanted see it had to get ready. That's where John came in.

John the Baptist invited people to a baptism of repentance. Repentance means more than just feeling sorry for the bad things you've done. Instead, it means searching your life for where you have gone off track, stopping that behavior or pattern, turning around, and then going in the other direction. This is a great way to deal with any regret you carry from your backstory. To be free from it requires first acknowledging that it is there, and then turning around and walking in the other direction. Is there anything you need to turn and walk away from in order to be ready for what God is going to do next in your life?

❀ Is there anything in your past you need to leave behind?

❀ What could make that difficult? What could make it easy?

❀ Pray. God is near.

❀ Day 4

MATTHEW 1:20-23

Now when Joseph had decided to act on his instincts, a messenger of the Lord came to him in a dream.

Messenger of the Lord: Joseph, son of David, do not be afraid to wed Mary *and bring her into your home and family* as your wife. *She did not sneak off and sleep with someone else*—rather, she conceived the baby she now carries through the miraculous won-derworking of the Holy Spirit. She will have a son, and you will name Him Jesus, *which means "the Lord saves,"* because this Jesus is the per-son who will save *all of* His people from sin.

Years and years ago, *Isaiah*, a prophet of Israel, foretold the story
of Mary, Joseph, and Jesus:

A virgin will conceive and bear a Son,
and His name will be Immanuel
(which is a Hebrew name that means "God with us").

Read the scripture for today and consider:

❖ Who chose Jesus' name?

❖ Is there anything that makes you wonder if Jesus' names have
a backstory?

Both of the names given in this passage have a connection to the
Hebrew Bible. The first, Jesus, is a cognate of Joshua. In the Old
Testament, Joshua led Israel out of the desert and into the promised land. God kept his promise through Joshua and what he did
through Jesus was similar and yet much, much bigger.

The other name given is Immanuel. This is a reference to Isaiah
7:14, when God assured the king that he cared for his people even

when they were being threatened. Jesus' name, Immanuel, is meant to evoke that whole story and communicate again that what God did through Jesus was both similar and much, much bigger.

⊛ Can you think of examples where Jesus acted to save people during his ministry?

⊛ Can you think of examples where Jesus protected people during his ministry?

⊛ How did both of these names come together on the cross?

⊛ What does your name mean? Are any parts of your character revealed in your name?

CHARACTERS

INTRODUCTION

Good stories have good characters. We recognize good characters because we can relate to them. Whenever we empathize with a protagonist or antagonist in a novel or movie, it is because the storyteller has developed that character well. However, we usually access a story through only one character's perspective. This person is called the main character and we see everything that happens through his eyes.

Lately, there has been a movement to retell some familiar and famous stories by viewing them from the perspective of a different character in the narrative. These novels, musicals, and movies have become wildly popular and suggest that maybe you would see things differently if you came at the event from another perspective.

The same could be said of the characters in our lives as well.

Supporting characters in the stories of our lives are often the instigators of change and growth in us. We need *them* in order to become what God wants *us* to be. So, every David needs a Jonathan, someone who will be our best friend through thick and thin. We all need a Nathan, someone to confront us in our sin and brokenness. More than likely, we will also deal with a Saul, someone we consider an enemy and who may be out to get us.

Your perspective may not be the only one worth considering. As you reflect this week on the characters in your story, think about the role you might play in their stories as well. How does you community shape you, positively and negatively? Where are your areas of conflict? And how might God use all these relationships toward one big, good end?

CHECKING IN

Last week, the "Experiments in Story" section invited you to explore the concept of backstory by observing it in popular media (movies, TV, books, etc.). Did you learn anything about backstory that you would like to share? How did your observations about backstory help you understand how to tell your own story more effectively?

STUDYING THE STORY
THE LIFE OF DAVID, PART 2

"Studying the Story" this week invites you to observe key character relationships in an infamous story from David's life: his encounter with Bathsheba.

Read **2 Samuel 11–12** out loud in a group. After you do, consider the following questions:

1. Who is main character in the story? Why did you answer the way you did?

2. The story is about an event in the life of David. From his perspective, what role did each of the following people play in his story?

   ▣ Bathsheba

   ▣ Nathan

   ▣ Solomon

   ▣ God

3. What role did David play in their stories?

4. Does looking at this story through the perspective of each person change how you read the story?

WATCH THE DVD

Watch *Session #2: Characters*. When the DVD ends, give everyone a moment to reflect and jot down one or two things that they learned, disagreed with, or found surprising.

GROUP DISCUSSION

First Impressions

Before everyone shares in the large group, turn to one or two people next to you and finish this sentence, "After watching the video about *Characters*, one question I have is . . ."

Community Reflections

1. Go around the group and have everyone share their name and one of their favorite fictional characters.

2. Len says, "Every one of us needs a Nathan" in our lives. What does he mean by this? Do you think he's right? Why or why not?

3. Is it easy or difficult to find God in your failure?

4. Have you ever seen God use your failure to bring about something good in your life? If so, when?

5. When the story of David and Bathsheba is brought up, Chris indicates that he would like to see the story explored from her perspective. How does seeing an event through someone else's eyes change your perspective on it?

6. How does God use the other characters in our story "as his hands and feet?"

7. Have you ever seen yourself as a character in someone else's story? What is that like?

8. In the video, Ben says, "God uses frustration to shape a vision." What do you think he means? Is conflict always negative? How can conflict shape our stories?

9. How do you see social media working against our ability to connect deeply with one another? How do you see social media *helping* us connect deeply with each other?

10. Len says that our social media makes us hunger more and more for face-to-face relationships but that the church is not poised to do this well because it is a place of doctrine. What does he mean by this? Do you think he's right?

EXPERIMENTS IN STORY

This week's session is all about characters and the role they play in good stories. For "Experiments in Story" this week you are invited to reflect on the key characters in your own story.

Imagine your life as an unfolding narrative and select three people who have been significant in shaping your story so far. Write down their names in your journal, and after each name, make a few notes about why that person is important to you. Consider whether that person is a positive or negative influence. Explain your answers.

Now write their names down again.

This time consider who you are in *their* stories. Make a few notes about how you imagine you might fit in with the unfolding narrative of *their* lives. Are you a good influence on them?

Make a note of anything you learned and be prepared to share during the next session.

EXPLORING THE STORY FURTHER

 *Day 1*

1 SAMUEL 19:1–3

Saul ordered his son Jonathan and all his servants *to figure out a way to kill David*, but Jonathan was very fond of David.

Jonathan *(warning David)*: My father wants you dead. Watch out tomorrow morning. Think of a safe place to hide that nobody knows about. I will go into the field near where you are hiding, and I will speak on your behalf to my father. If I learn anything, I will tell you.

Read the scripture for today and consider:

- Have you ever felt like someone was out to get you? How did that make you feel and what did you do about it?

At this point in the story, David has been anointed the true king of Israel. Saul, the reigning king, mentally unraveled and tried to murder David. It was an intense conflict that must have been painful, considering David's close relationship with Saul's son Jonathan. In your life, there may be people who are out to get you.

They may not be trying to literally murder you, but like Saul, they might be relentless in their attacks and even try to get others to do their dirty work for them.

We would do well to observe how David navigated these conditions. He never took matters into his own hands. He never plotted a preemptive strike or tried to turn Jonathan against his father. Instead, he trusted God for his care, protection, and sustenance. This doesn't mean David did not bemoan his condition. The Psalms are full of places where David cried out for justice (Ps. 56) and even demanded that God destroy his enemies (Ps. 143:12). The important thing is that he left it all in God's hands. He told the truth about what he felt in prayer, but he left the justice to the Lord. Can you do the same? How can you follow David's example in dealing with your enemies?

⌘ Who are your enemies and why are they your enemies?

⌘ What does it mean for you to trust God to do justice?

⌘ Are you "the enemy" in any one else's story right now? If so, what can you learn from this situation in 1 Samuel?

▨ How does Jesus' teaching to "pray for those . . . who persecute you" (Matt. 5:44) apply to your enemies?

Day 2

1 SAMUEL 18:1–4

By the time David had finished speaking to Saul, *Saul's son* Jonathan was bound to David *in friendship,* and Jonathan loved David as he loved himself. Saul took David *into his service* on that day and would not let him return to his father's home. And Jonathan made a covenant with David because he loved him as he loved himself. He took off the robe he wore and gave it to David, and also his armor, sword, bow, and belt, *symbolically transferring to David his right to ascend the throne.*

Read the scriptures for today and consider:

▨ Who are a few of your best friends today? What makes them good friends?

The relationship between David and Jonathan is one of the most beautiful depictions of friendship found in the Bible. What makes it so compelling is not simply the depth of affection the two friends have for each other, but it is the way they put their love for each other into action. We get a small snapshot of this in the reading for this morning.

Jonathan is the political heir to the throne of Israel, but David is God's choice. Jonathan knows this, so he makes the incredibly difficult choice to lay down his rights and give away his claim on the throne to David. He does so because, as the text repeats, he "loved David as he loved himself." His love for David is expressed in selfless action. Our closest friendships will have markers of this same dynamic.

What makes a friendship strong is a mix of affection, vulnerability, and sacrifice. We see this between David and Jonathan in the scripture today. Affection is present in the way Jonathan loves David as himself. Vulnerability is pictured in the way he takes off his armor and weapons. Sacrifice is demonstrated when Jonathan hands over his right to the throne. How much affection, vulnerability, and sacrifice are present in your friendships? How much do you expect from your friends and how much do you bring to the table yourself? What is one way you can put love-in-action in your significant friendships? Exploring questions like these will bring more intentionality to our friendships and open up their power in our story.

▓ Which of these three (affection, vulnerability, and sacrifice) do you value most in your friendships?

◈ Which of the three do you find the most challenging to express to your friends?

◈ Is there one of the three that is more difficult to accept than the others?

◈ Think of at least one friendship in your life that is meaningful. Consider what makes it meaningful to you and give God thanks for that friendship in your life.

Day 3

2 SAMUEL 12:1–7A

The Eternal One sent *the prophet* Nathan to visit David. Nathan came to him and told him *a story*.

Nathan: Two men lived in the same city. One was *quite* rich and the other *quite* poor; the rich man's wealth included *livestock with many flocks and herds*, but the poor man owned only one little ewe lamb. He bought it and raised it in his family, with his children, *like a pet*. It used to eat what *little* food he had, drink from his *meager* cup, and snuggle against him. It was like a daughter to him.

Now a traveler came to the city *to visit* the rich man. *To offer a proper welcome*, the rich man knew he needed to fix a meal, but he did not want to take one of the animals from his flocks and herds. So instead he stole the poor man's ewe lamb and had it killed and cooked for his guest.

Nathan stood back, waiting for the king's verdict. David grew very angry at the *rich* man. *It was his royal duty to protect the poor and establish justice.*

David: As the Eternal One lives, the *rich* man who did this deserves to die. *At the least*, he will restore that lamb four times over because he acted without pity.

Nathan: You are that man!

Read the scripture for today and consider:

⊗ Is it difficult or easy for you to receive correction? Why?

One of the hardest things to do is admit when you are wrong. Demonstrating weakness can threaten your conviction that you've got it all together. However, you needn't fear correction because God will never use it to shame or condemn you. Instead, God brings correction into your life to produce a new future.

You can choose to work with or against God in this endeavor. You can admit your failure, turn from it, and start fresh, or you can deny it and stay exactly where you are. The choice is yours—just like it was for David. The reading today ends with Nathan saying, "You are the man!" What did David do next? What should he have done next, or more importantly, what would *you* do next?

▧ Who is a Nathan-type person in your life?

▧ What is your immediate reaction to being confronted with your faults?

▧ How do you deal with failure? Do you see it as an opportunity for God to demonstrate his love or his judgment?

 # Day 4

1 SAMUEL 13:13-14

Samuel: That was a foolish thing, Saul. You have not kept the commandment that the Eternal, your True God, gave to you. He was willing to establish your kingdom over Israel for all time, but now your kingdom, *your dynasty,* will not last. He has found a man who seeks His will and has appointed him king over all the people *instead of you* because you have not kept to what the Eternal One commanded.

Read the scripture for today and consider:

What does it mean to you to be a person "after God's own heart"?

The text today is an invitation to look at David's life through the eyes of the main character in the biblical story: God. Today's portion of 1 Samuel includes the very famous verse where Samuel told Saul that Yahweh had selected a new king for Israel who was "after his own heart." What does such a description even mean?

Simply put, for David to be "a man after God's own heart" meant that somewhere at the core of his being, David cared about the things God cares about. Deep within himself, he believed in God and trusted what God was doing. This was primarily revealed not in the way David made good choices, but instead how he dealt with the bad ones. When confronted with his sin, David honestly and openly repented. This was unbecoming behavior for a king in his day, but David was showing us a kingdom that is not of this world. David missed the mark many times and in many ways, but his responses to his failures revealed God's heart.

⊠ What does it mean for you to be a person "after God's own heart"?

⊠ Is it easy or difficult for you to receive the grace to fail?

⊠ Have you learned anything new about God's kingdom from the session this week?

PLOT

INTRODUCTION

The stories we resonate with the most all have one thing in common: the characters in them change. The arc in a story where this kind of change occurs is called "The Plot." For our purposes, the plot is the movement of transformation that occurs in a character from the beginning to the end of a story. It is the growth, change, and development we observe in a story's characters. What drives this plot in every great story is conflict. So, whether it comes from a broken relationship, the consequences of bad behavior, or a tragic turn of events, the plot of a story focuses on the struggle that leads to growth in the characters.

This is true in our stories as well. Conflict and struggle are what drive change in us. However, in the midst of such contention, it can be easy to lose our perspective. Our pain and anxiety become all-consuming and we forget that conflict is not the end of our story—resurrection is. Remembering this helps us step back and take the long view of life. It helps us remember that our current place of failure and pain is not the end, but might in fact just be the middle—the middle of an arc of growth. This is because, as Christians, we are living a plot that uses weakness to disclose God's strength and that takes death and brings new life from it.

This is what we will explore during this session.

How do you tend to perceive conflict and challenge when you first encounter it? Does it make you want to give up? Give in? Fight back? Bring these reflections to the session this week and look for the ways God might be using conflict in your life to mold you into the image of Jesus.

CHECKING IN

Last week the "Experiments in Story" section invited you to imagine your life as an unfolding narrative and then to choose three people who have been significant in your story.

What did you learn? Who is one of your people? Were they a positive or negative influence? Who did you think you were in *their* story? Using the notes in your journal, share a few things you learned.

STUDYING THE STORY

THE LIFE OF DAVID, PART 3

"Studying the Story" this week invites you to observe the plot of David's life. David had highs and lows in his life, but through it all he deeply trusted God. Read the following passages of Scripture out loud, then reflect together on the questions that follow.

1 Samuel 16:6–13 (David anointed King)

- How did God's criteria for Israel's king differ from what was expected?

- Is this a high or low point in David's plot?

1 Samuel 17:1–51 (David and Goliath)

- How did David grow in this conflict?

- Is this a high or low point in David's story?

2 Samuel 12:1–7 (David and Nathan)

- What has happened leading up to this event?

- Is this a high or low point in David's life?

2 Samuel 17:1–4 (Pursued by Absalom)

- Does this sound like a high or low point in David's life?

2 Samuel 6: 12–19

◉ How do highs and lows mix in this text?

Each of these events is taken from the whole story of David's life. Now consider the story of his failure with Bathsheba. Where does this story fit in to the whole arc of David's life? Does looking at his whole life change the way you see that one event? Does the long view of David's life affect the way you see consequences of his behavior with Bathsheba? Why or why not?

WATCH THE DVD

Watch *Session #3: Plot*. When the DVD ends, give everyone a moment to reflect and jot down one or two things that they learned, disagreed with, or found surprising.

GROUP DISCUSSION

We have fewer questions this week because the group time invites more personal storytelling.

First Impressions

Before everyone shares in the large group, turn to one or two people next to you and finish this sentence, "After watching the video about *Plot* one question I have is . . ."

Community Reflections

1. Who is your favorite villain of all time? What makes this person your favorite?

2. What do we learn from the life of David about getting our stories back on track when they've gone astray?

3. Do you agree that taking the "long view" and seeing our lives as having story arcs helps us make sense of our failures and struggles? Why or why not?

4. Len suggests that "the very best in me is just a hairsbreadth from the very worst in me." What do you think he means by this? Do you agree?

5. Ben opens the video by suggesting that what we love about stories is watching the "transformation of characters." We relate to this because it is what happens in our lives. Can you think of a time when transformation took place in your life? If so, would you share it with the group?

6. Pete tells a heartbreaking story to conclude the video. It's about losing a baby and how sometimes stories don't resolve like we imagined they would. Have you ever had an experience like the one he described? Where did you find God in that?

7. Is it hard to believe God is with us when our stories do not resolve like we wanted them to? Why or why not?

EXPERIMENTS IN STORY

This session is all about how the plot of our story is built around the conflicts that change us. The video and the study guide suggest that we need to take the long view of our lives. We can then evaluate our struggles and pain in light of the bigger story. However, this means at some point reflecting on what will happen at the ends of our lives.

Your "Experiments in Story" this week is to attend a funeral. If you cannot find a funeral open to the public, read a funeral liturgy or service. When you do, consider the following:

⊛ What do funerals teach me about how I want to live?

⊛ What does it mean to both live and die well?

⊛ What makes a "good life" good?

How am I aiming toward honoring God by trusting him to carry me through life's difficulties?

Make a note of anything you learned and be prepared to share during the next session.

EXPLORING THE STORY FURTHER

This week's set of daily readings will explore the story of Joseph and his plot as referenced by Pete in the video.

Day 1

GENESIS 37:2-4

Here now is the story of Jacob and his family:

Joseph, when he was a young man of 17, often shepherded the flocks along with his brothers. *One day* as he was with Bilhah's and Zilpah's sons (his half-brothers), he decided to report back to their father about things they were doing wrong. Now Israel loved Joseph more than any of his other children because he came along when he was an old man. So Israel presented Joseph with a special robe he had made for him—*a spectacularly colorful robe with long sleeves* in it. But when his brothers saw that their father loved him more than the rest, they grew to hate him and couldn't *find it in themselves to* speak to him without resentment or argument.

─────────────────✕─────────────────

Read the scripture for today and consider:

◈ Why did Joseph's father like him the best?

◈ How did this favoritism affect the family?

The story of Joseph really starts here. We have all the characters introduced, and now we're going to see what motivates the conflict in the story. From this initial description you could make the case that things are going to go really well for Joseph in life. He seems to have had an advantage. Joseph had, in many ways, what we all want, including special status.

But look at the effects.

Dark clouds gather in verse 4. The storyteller wants us to understand that this special treatment caused all sorts of pain, hate, and jealousy just under the surface. Have you ever seen this happen in a family or group of friends? When was that? Have you ever seen special treatment of one person cause resentment in everybody else?

It didn't work out for Joseph, as we will see later, which begs the question: Do you think special treatment works out for anybody?

❀ Which of the main characters (Joseph, Jacob/Israel, Joseph's brothers) do you relate to most? Why?

❀ What effects do you see from special treatment and favoritism in our world today?

❀ What is Jesus' response to favoritism like this?

❀ *Day 2*

GENESIS 37:23-28

When Joseph arrived, they ripped his robe off of him—the fancy, colorful robe he always wore *that his father had made for him*, and they threw him into the pit. Now this pit happened to be an empty *cistern*; there was no water in it.

Then they sat down to eat. Soon they looked up and saw a caravan of Ishmaelite traders approaching from Gilead. Their camels were loaded with gum, balm, and a fragrant resin; and they were on their way down to Egypt with their goods.

Judah *(to his brothers)*: What profit will it be for us if we just kill our brother and conceal the crime? Come on, let's sell him to the Ishmaelites instead. We won't have to lay a hand on him then. He is, after all, our brother, our own flesh *and blood*.

All of the brothers agreed. As the Midianite traders were passing by, they brought Joseph up out of the pit and sold him to the Ishmaelites for about eight ounces of silver, *the usual price of young male slaves*. The traders set off with Joseph in the direction of Egypt.

Read the scripture for today and consider:

❊ What is the connection between resentment, hatred, and violence? Why do you think they go together so often?

In the plot of Joseph's life, this is a definite point of conflict. Joseph's own brothers betrayed and abused him, then sold him to slave traders who took him away to Eygpt. Could things get any worse? As you might guess, the answer is: absolutely.

However, this is where the concept of plot is so challenging in Joseph's story. At this point, the conflict is in full swing and the storyteller suddenly pivots the spotlight onto us, the readers, and asks, "Do you really believe God could bring something good out of a situation like this? Do you? Just how good do you really think God is?"

Challenging questions, aren't they? How would you answer today?

- If you were Joseph, how do you think you would answer those questions?

- Is it difficult or easy for you to trust God's goodness in the midst of calamity?

- What role does faith play in helping to answer these questions?

- Pray. God is near.

 # Day 3

GENESIS 40:9-23

So the chief cupbearer told Joseph his dream.

Cupbearer: In my dream, there was a vine in front of me, and on the vine were three branches. As soon as it budded, its blossoms opened up and its clusters ripened into grapes. Pharaoh's cup was in my hand, and I took the grapes and pressed them into Pharaoh's cup, and then I placed the cup into Pharaoh's hand.

Joseph: This is what your dream means: the three branches are three days. Within three days, Pharaoh will lift up your head and restore you to your office; you will place Pharaoh's cup in his hand, just as you used to do when you were his cupbearer.

But I *ask one thing*. Remember me when things are going well for you. *If you have the opportunity,* do me a favor and mention me to Pharaoh. *Perhaps he will* get me out of this place. You see I was stolen from the land of *my people* the Hebrews, and I've done nothing to deserve being thrown into this pit.

When the chief baker saw that the cupbearer received such a good interpretation, he told Joseph his dream *as well*.

Baker: I've also had a dream: There were three baskets of *fine* cakes *stacked* on my head. In the upper basket, there were all sorts of baked goods for Pharaoh, but the birds *swooped down and* kept eating Pharaoh's food out of the basket on my head.

Joseph: This is what your dream means: the three baskets are three days. Within three days, Pharaoh will lift your head and remove it *from you*. He will impale your body on a tree and vultures will *swoop down and* eat the flesh from your bones.

On the third day, which also happened to be Pharaoh's birthday, he prepared a *huge* feast for all of his servants. As they were gathered together, he lifted up the head of the chief cupbearer and restored him to his former office. *That day* the cupbearer resumed placing the cup in Pharaoh's hand. But Pharaoh lifted off the head of the chief baker and impaled him *on a tree for the birds*, just as Joseph had interpreted. *Sadly* the chief cupbearer did not remember Joseph *at this time*; instead, he forgot all about him.

Read the scripture for today and consider:

* If you were Joseph, how would you respond to the chief cupbearer forgetting you?

Disappointment can be very difficult to deal with, especially when things seem to work against you over and over. In the story of Joseph it just seemed to be one thing after another. Joseph was betrayed by his brothers, falsely accused of rape, wrongfully imprisoned, and when there seemed to be a glimmer of hope (the cupbearer putting in a good word for him), the light was snuffed out.

Have you ever felt this way?

Seeing how Joseph lived a life of hope and trust in the face of constant disappointment is inspiring and challenging. It's challenging because we know that place of disillusionment and understand how hard it is not to fold into self-pity or anger. It's inspiring because we know the end of the story. We know God is going to rescue Joseph; he just hasn't done it yet. Do we believe the same is true of God in our own times of frustration?

◈ Has there ever been a time when you felt like Joseph?

◈ Is it easy or difficult to take the "long view" of life during those times?

◈ Is it easy or difficult for you to connect with God during experiences of disappointment? Why did you answer the way you did?

◈ Pray. God is near.

Day 4

GENESIS 50:15–21

When Joseph's brothers began to realize *the implications of* their father's death, Joseph's brothers *began to worry.*

Joseph's Brothers: What if Joseph still bears a grudge *in some way* against us and decides to pay us back in full for all of the wrong we did to him?

So they sent a message to Joseph.

Joseph's Brothers' Message: Your father gave us this instruction before he died. He told us to say to you, "Please, I beg you. Forgive the crime of your brothers and the sins they committed against you. They were wrong to treat you so badly." So please do *what your father asked and* forgive the crime that we, the servants of the God of your father, committed against you.

Joseph cried when they spoke these words to him. And his brothers approached and fell at his feet.

Joseph's Brothers: Look! We are your slaves.

Joseph: Don't be afraid. Am I *to judge* instead of God? *It is not my place.* Even though you intended to harm me, God intended it only for good, and through me, He preserved the lives of countless people, as He is still doing today. So don't worry. I will provide for you *myself*—for you and your children.

So Joseph reassured them and continued to speak kindly to them.

⊞ What do you think it means when Joseph says, "Even though you intended to harm me, God intended it only for good"?

⊞ Does a phrase like this bring you comfort or tension?

Here at the end of Joseph's story we see redemption and salvation. Because of Joseph and his position, his entire family (all of Israel) was saved. They made it through the famine and had plenty.

Although Joseph's plot was full of pain of contention, God used it to bring about something good. Joseph saw that, even though human sin is real and affected him deeply (he was betrayed, enslaved, falsely accused, etc.) God can be trusted. There is nothing so horrible that God can't bring something good from it.

⊞ How can Joseph's story be an example of trusting God's plot for our lives?

▦ Is this how you see suffering and misfortune in your life?

▦ If you were Joseph, would it be easy or difficult to take "the long view" of what God was doing in your life?

METAPHOR

INTRODUCTION

The best teachers always teach with story and metaphor. This is because metaphors accomplish more than simple statements or instructions can. They give us a picture of another world and help us visualize the invisible. This is part of the reason why Jesus taught in parables. The metaphors he employed to describe God's kingdom were designed to open the only faculty designed to apprehend the kingdom of God: the human heart. Metaphors can do that. They can open our hearts to God's new world and can inspire us to make his kingdom known here on earth as it is in heaven.

We see a powerful example of this heart-opening reality in 2 Samuel 12:1–14. When Nathan confronted David about his sin with Bathsheba, he did not begin with a direct accusation. One can only imagine how effective that might have been. David was the king! He was acting well within his political rights to kill Uriah and take the man's wife as his own. What could be argued about his behavior from a political perspective? The answer is: very little. So, Nathan, as a prophet of God, told David a story about injustice regarding a man, his neighbor, and their sheep. When David realized the story was about him, his heart opened to God's perspective and it cut him to the core. This is the power of metaphor, and we will be exploring it further during this session.

Those who tell the best stories are the ones who shape the culture. This is why totalitarian regimes always censor poets and artists first. They don't want someone else telling the truth in a way that will give people hope. Stories and metaphors are powerful. How can metaphors help us understand God's story better, and how can they help us tell our stories in ways that open hearts and change the world?

CHECKING IN

In last week's "Experiments in Story" you were invited to attend a funeral and reflect on the experience.

Explore with the group:

◉ Was anyone able to get to an actual funeral? What was your experience like?

◉ If you did not get to an actual funeral, what funeral service did you read over?

◈ Did this exploration of death teach you anything about how you want to live?

◈ Would anyone like to share how they answered any of the reflection questions from the end of last week's "Experiments in Story"?

◈ Are there other reflections anyone would like to share with the group?

STUDYING THE STORY
THE LIFE OF DAVID, PART 4

This week we return to the story when Nathan rebuked David.
Read 2 Samuel 12:1–13 and consider:

◈ Did you hear anything new in the story this time through?

How did Nathan use metaphor to get David's attention?

How did David connect the dots between the story of the lamb and his own behavior?

What made Nathan's metaphor work?

What is the right way to use metaphor in Christian community?

What is the wrong way to use metaphor in Christian community?

WATCH THE DVD

Watch *Session 4: Metaphor*. When the DVD ends, give everyone a moment to reflect and jot down one or two things that they learned, disagreed with, or found surprising.

GROUP DISCUSSION

First Impressions

Before everyone shares in the large group, turn to one or two people next to you and finish this sentence, "After watching the video about *Metaphor* one question I have is . . ."

Community Reflections

1. When you read the Bible, are there any stories that you picture like a movie? If so, which ones?

2. Len says he sees himself as a "story catcher" more than a story-teller because, "You can't tell a story until you've found a story." What do you think this means?

3. As a group, develop a working definition of the word "metaphor." What do you think is the relationship between metaphor and story?

4. Len coins the term "narraphor," the blending and cross-pollination of metaphors and stories. How can you (or have you) used narraphor to tell your own story?

5. How is Nathan's story about the two men and the lamb an example of metaphor presenting, as Chris says in the video, "the world as it is versus the world as it should be"?

6. What do we do with such tension when we cannot resolve it? Is it okay to try to resolve the tension?

7. Ginny says, "I am a story" and that what God is doing in her is her story. What do you think she means by this? Do you see yourself as a story?

8. Do you see God's activity from Bible times until the present day as an ongoing and unfolding story? Is it easy or difficult to see yourself as part of that story?

9. During the closing segment of the video, Ben suggests that the seasons of our lives, like a book or movie, can have a genre. Do you agree? What genre do you think you are living right now? Is that the genre God wants you to live?

10. How can you tell the difference between the times we are to act creatively to change the genre of our story and the times we are supposed to just let our stories unfold? Are those really the only two options?

EXPERIMENTS IN STORY

When metaphors are used in the Bible, they are built around common images, experiences, and stories with which the original audience was familiar. For your "Experiment in Story" this week you are invited to write a metaphor that illustrates your story.

Think about something you are learning or wondering right now. Or, consider a recent lesson you have learned about God or life in general. Then think through how to recast that story, learning experience, or event using a metaphor. Use a contemporary story (like a movie) if it helps or make up your own.

Spend two of the next five days working at this and come to the next session ready to share your metaphor.

EXPLORING THE STORY FURTHER

This week's set of daily readings will explore metaphors from Psalms and the teachings of Jesus. Each day you will be invited to recast the metaphor using images from today's culture. Jot down what you come up with and be prepared to share during the next session.

 *Day 1*

MATTHEW 13:44

The kingdom of heaven is like a treasure that is hidden in a field. A *crafty* man found the treasure buried there and buried it again *so no one would know where it was*. Thrilled, he went off and sold everything he had, and then he came back and bought the field *with the hidden treasure part of the bargain*.

Read the scripture for today and consider:

What is the kingdom of heaven?

What questions does this metaphor leave you with?

In Jesus' day, saying the "kingdom of heaven" was the same thing as saying "the kingdom of God." Using the word "heaven" was a way for observant Jews to honor the name of God without taking it in vain. However, whether the word "God" or "heaven" was used, the audience would have known exactly what Jesus was referring to. God's kingdom is the place and space where God runs the show. It is the domain where God's will is done and things are as God wants them to be. Jesus expected God's kingdom to be made known on earth as it was in heaven.

So, what of the field?

Well, in Jesus' day there were numerous expectations about how God's kingdom would come. Many anticipated it would be a grand spectacle that was huge and impossible to miss. That's what's so confounding about the field. What Jesus teaches is that God's kingdom is something you *can* miss if you're not paying attention. Like a treasure hidden in a field, if you're moving too quickly, not paying attention, or simply too determined to find it your own way, you might miss it altogether. Finding this treasure, as it turns out, takes knowing where to look.

Well, why doesn't he just say this? Well he does . . . with a metaphor, and here we are talking about it two thousand years later. The kingdom of heaven is best described in metaphor—like a treasure in a field.

How can you apply this parable to your own life with God?

⊗ Where is it wise to look for God's kingdom and where would you miss it?

⊗ How would you retell this parable to make the same point using the signs and symbols of today's culture?

 Day 2

MATTHEW 13:31–32

Jesus told them another parable.

Jesus: The kingdom of heaven is like a mustard seed, which a sower took and planted in his field. Mustard seeds are minute, tiny—but the seeds grow into trees. Flocks of birds can come and build their nests in the branches.

Read the scripture for today and consider:

⊗ What do you think Jesus is teaching about God's kingdom?

What questions does this metaphor leave you with?

We live in a culture that lauds monumental achievement and celebrity. The stories we tell to inspire our children in school are of remarkable individuals who beat the odds in order to accomplish great things. We do this to inspire kids to dream big. While this is not a bad thing, there can be unintended consequences.

The parable about God's kingdom above is another metaphor. It is one of many found in Matthew 13. In the parable, Jesus compared God's kingdom to something small: a mustard seed. He included the detail that it was the smallest seed that a gardener would use (which is helpful for non-agrarian types) but pointed out that the mustard plant could grow to be the biggest thing in the garden.

What was Jesus getting at?

God's kingdom best takes root not in our herculean efforts or widespread influence but in small, unnoticed things. However, we can be confident that, when planted, those unseen seeds of goodness will grow and grow until they are strong enough to offer refuge to others. This good news reminds us that *everything* we do matters. So, every kind word, every work of generosity, every fair act of business or trade, each has a place in building God's kingdom here on earth as it is in heaven. They are like mustard seeds that start small but become like the biggest plant in the garden.

How do you think this parable is good news for Christians today?

How would you retell this parable using the signs and symbols of today's culture to make the same point?

 *Day 3*

JEREMIAH 2:13

My people are guilty of two evils:
They have abandoned Me, the spring of living waters;
And instead, they have settled for dead and stagnant water
from cracked, leaky cisterns of their own making.

Read the scripture for today and consider:

What are the two sins God declares his people have committed?

❋ What is a cistern?

Many of the metaphors the prophets employed used actual places in the region as their reference points. Jeremiah did this when he referenced "living water" and "cisterns." His metaphor refers to three things which are related.

First, he makes the distinction between "living" water and other kinds of water. Living water in the Hebrew Bible was any water that flowed on its own. So, rain falling from the sky, a river or stream, or a waterfall, would all be considered living water. Water, once collected in a bucket or trough was no longer living water. Living water had to be moving.

The second reference he makes is to an actual place in the Judean wilderness called Ein Gedi. The desert outside Jerusalem is a very rugged and dry place. It is a taxing environment for any living thing to inhabit. However, on its edge near the Dead Sea, there is a huge oasis formed around a spring that shoots out of the side of a mountain to create a giant waterfall. This waterfall is called Ein Gedi. Ein Gedi is where David hid from Saul in 1 Samuel 24:1–3, and some believe it is the very picture of "living water" Jeremiah is referring to above.[1]

---

1 Ray Vander Laan, *Echoes of His Presence*. With Judith Markham. (Grand Rapids: Zondervan, 1998), 109–122.

The last reference is to a cistern, which is a large clay pot or barrel used for collecting water. These were common in the region because water was so scarce. A cistern allowed you to collect water and hold it until you needed it. But people were not the only creatures looking for water. Many animals would find a cisterns someone had dug and, in their desperation for water, climb in to get a drink. If the walls of the cistern were too steep for the animal to get back out, they would get trapped and die there. This would poison the water and make you sick if you drank it.

This context puts God's frustration with his people into perspective. They had left Ein Gedi, the source of living, fresh, and life-sustaining water in order to dig cisterns that would make them sick. It is an extremely evocative image that prompts people to ask, "Am I drinking anything that is making me sick today?"

⊕ Is there a cistern you are drinking from today that is making you sick? What will it mean to return to God, the source of living water?

⊕ How could you recast this metaphor using the signs and symbols of today's culture?

Day 4

So woe to you, teachers of the law and Pharisees. You hypocrites! You tithe from your *luxuries and your spices, giving away a tenth* of your mint, your dill, and your cumin. But you have ignored the essentials of the law: justice, mercy, faithfulness. It is practice of the latter that makes sense of the former. You *hypocritical*, blind leaders. You spoon a fly from your soup and swallow a camel.

Woe to you, teachers of the law and Pharisees, you hypocrites! You remove fine layers of film and dust from the outside of a cup or bowl, but you leave the inside full of greed and covetousness and self-indulgence. You blind Pharisee—can't you see that if you clean the inside of the cup, the outside will be clean too?

Woe to you, teachers of the law and Pharisees, you hypocrites! You are like a grave that has been whitewashed. You look beautiful on the outside, but on the inside you are full of moldering bones and decaying rot. You appear, at first blush, to be righteous, *selfless, and pure*; but on the inside you are polluted, sunk in hypocrisy and confusion and lawlessness.

Read the scripture for today and consider:

⬡ Jesus used three metaphors in the text today. What was his point with each one?

⬡ Do you think there is there a common theme between the three metaphors?

In our section of the gospel of Matthew today Jesus let Israel's religious leaders have it. You can almost feel his frustration as he laid out the woes, each building on the other. The leaders responsible for guiding God's people into his justice, beauty, and love had missed the point. They made God's law a set of hoops to jump through instead of mastering "the more important matters" of doing justice and mercy.

To illustrate this sad state of affairs, Jesus used a series of metaphors. In the first he employed an outrageous word picture that ironically contrasted someone straining out a gnat while swallowing a camel. He followed that up with two more contrasting inner realities with outward appearances. Like dishes that only get cleaned on the outside or a beautifully painted grave, Jesus said these religious leaders look great on the outside, but are rotten, filthy, and full of death on the inside.

No small talk, huh? So what do we do with these words today?

First, consider how you hear Jesus' words this week. Are they words of comfort or challenge? Then, remember that Jesus only accosted Israel's leaders because they were unwilling to listen to his correction. He didn't lambaste them because they made a mistake, and he won't do that to you either. As Jesus' words move you to change, then these metaphors can become a gateway to freedom and peace, not condemnation.

⊛ How could the metaphors Jesus used be "good news" today?

⊛ What is one way these woes challenge the contemporary church?

⊛ What is one way these woes challenge you?

⊛ Pray. God is near.

NARRATIVE

INTRODUCTION

Have you ever turned on the television to find a movie you love already playing? If you started watching it right then and there, then you have already experienced the power of narrative. A narrative, for our purposes, is different than the plot. The plot is the conflict that drives the story, but the narrative is the story itself. It's the one, overarching tale of a book, movie, or television show from beginning to end. All of the smaller scenes of the story exist to serve it. A narrative, then, is why you can jump into a movie that is halfway through. You already know the whole story and understand where it fits in the entire narrative.

In this session we will explore how the Bible is a grand narrative as well. It is not an anthology full of lots of different, quasi-related stories. Instead, the Bible is one massive, grand narrative that carries all the way through, from Genesis to Revelation. This doesn't mean, however, that we should expect the Bible to read like one of our novels. Its story isn't laid out in a neat timeline. Instead, like all great ancient writings, it moves in a spiral formation, giving us vignettes from the beginning, the middle, and end of the story, all along the way. This concept is developed further in the video.

However, that is what is so great about the Bible. It is constructed purposefully to draw us in. It invites us to find God in its narrative and then challenges us bring its story into our own lives. This means all our circumstances, choices, and decisions are part of, and can be seen in light of, God's grand story. No matter how good or bad things get, we are invited to trust that our story is still going somewhere good because it is part of God's narrative.

Which leaves the question, "Do you?" Do you trust God's story from Genesis to Revelation in such a way that no matter what life throws at you, you can trust that your story is still a good story? Or is that too difficult to accept? Bring these questions with you this week as we begin *Session #5: Narrative*.

CHECKING IN

Last week the "Experiments in Story" section invited you to write a metaphor describing your life with God or something you were learning about his kingdom.

- Share your metaphor (or one of the metaphors you recast from "Exploring the Story Further") with the group. Why did you choose the imagery that you did?

Also reflect:

◈ Was this an easy or difficult task?

◈ In your opinion, is learning to use metaphor a valuable skill to develop? Why or why not?

STUDYING THE STORY
THE LIFE OF DAVID, PART 5

The life of David is not a stand-alone story. It is part of the larger narrative of the whole Bible.

Read the following two texts aloud:

Genesis 3:1–6

Revelation 22:1–2

Ask the group:

◈ What is the connecting image between these two texts?

In the passages from Genesis and Revelation we get pictures of two different kinds of trees. The first is the tree of the knowledge of good and evil in the garden of Eden, which the humans ate from, bringing sin and death into creation. The second is the tree of life found in the new creation. Its leaves are for the healing of the nations.

We live in the time between these trees, and so did David. Evaluate David's life and story from the Bible that we have explored so far. How is it illustrative of both the first tree and the second?

WATCH THE DVD

Watch *Session 5: Narrative.* When the DVD ends, give everyone a moment to reflect and jot down one or two things that they learned, disagreed with, or found surprising.

GROUP DISCUSSION

First Impressions

Before everyone shares in the large group, turn to one or two people next to you and finish this sentence, "After watching the video about *Narrative* one question I have is . . ."

Community Reflections

1. What is one movie or novel that you can jump into at any point and still enjoy it?

2. Len says that in our culture we create identity in what we buy and what we wear. Do you recognize this? What does the term "identity" mean in this context? Do you agree with Len that consumer identity is one of the biggest threats to Christianity today?

3. Do you see your life as part of a story that you inherited? What is one way the story that has been passed on to you and has shaped you? What is one way you can learn from this story and not let it dictate bad patterns to you?

4. How do you respond to the claim that the Bible is one big story? Does that feel liberating or threatening?

5. Len says that the "authoritative word of God is the authoritative story of God. You can trust this story." What does he mean by this? Do you think he's right?

6. Have chapters and verses been a helpful addition to the Bible?

7. In your experience, is the Bible the greatest story ever told, or the greatest story *never* told?

8. Len suggests everyone ought to be able to tell the Biblical narrative as one story, Genesis to Revelation, in about ten minutes. Take the next ten minutes and, as a group, do just that. Afterward reflect on what this was like. Which parts did you know well? Which parts did you struggle with?

9. Ginny tells her story about wanting to be a choral teacher and ending up a songwriter instead. She says it was a lesson in trusting God and his story for her life. Is it easy or difficult for you to trust God with your life and your story? When things do not work out like you want them to, do you still see yourself as part of a good story?

EXPERIMENTS IN STORY

During the group discussion time, you were invited to tell the Biblical story in ten minutes. For this week's "Experiments in Story" you are invited to attempt this again on your own. Write down some notes on a piece of paper to help you present the story as a whole. Now, find a friend, roommate, or spouse who is not involved in this study and ask if you can present the story to them.

If you feel unfamiliar with the Bible, refer back to the Bible study for this week and use the daily readings below as hooks on which to hang your story.

When you are finished, reflect on the following questions:

⊗ Was this experiment easy or difficult?

⊗ Why did you choose the story points that you did?

⊗ Did you learn anything new about the biblical story as a result of this exercise?

Bring answers to these reflections to share in the group during the next session.

EXPLORING THE STORY FURTHER

Theologian and retired Anglican Bishop N. T. Wright pointed out in his book *The New Testament and the People of God* that we should approach the Bible as if it is a Five Act Play. He notes that the five elements of classic storytelling are present across the entire canon. Those five are,

1. The Introduction of the Characters,

2. Conflict,

3. Crescendo, (the interplay of between characters and the conflict which ratchets up to the . . .)

4. Climax, and finally,

5. Denouement (the out working of the results of the climax on the character's lives).

The Bible, Wright contends, plays these same beats, but the fifth act of the Bible is left incomplete. We know the end of the story and what happens in Acts 1—4, but the "middle" of Act 5 is unclear. Fleshing out this fifth act, he asserts, is the job of the church.[1]

Like actors in an unfinished play, we become so immersed in the Biblical narrative that we can "faithfully improvise" our way toward God's conclusion. The readings this week will illustrate each part of the five-act play and give a touchstone for each one through which we can see the big story of the Bible.

Day 1
Act 1: Characters

GENESIS 1:1

In the beginning, God created everything: the heavens *above* and the earth *below*.

GENESIS 1:31

Then God surveyed everything He had made, savoring *its beauty and appreciating* its goodness. Evening gave way to morning. That was day six.

---

1 N. T. Wright, *The New Testament and the People of God* (Minneapolis: Fortress).

GENESIS 2:15-17

The Eternal God placed the *newly made* man in the garden of Eden in order to work the ground and care for it. He made certain demands of the man *regarding life in the garden.*

God: Eat freely from any *and all* trees in the garden; I only require that you abstain from eating the fruit of *one tree*—the tree of the knowledge of good and evil. *Beware:* the day you eat the fruit of this tree, you will certainly die.

Read the scripture for today and consider:

◈ Who is the main character in the Bible?

◈ What is the backstory of this character?

God is the main character of the biblical story. In the beginning it's God who acted and created everything. However, it's important to note two things about God and what God intended with this creation project. First, notice that human beings were created to partner with God in taking the creation somewhere. We are not God's enemies in this story, nor are we his slaves. Our backstory with God is that we are meant to be partners and friends.

This brings up the second point. The arrangement between God and people is a good thing. The whole creation project begins with goodness—in fact, everything was very good. What's more, heaven (the realm of God's activity) and earth (ours) are all one. Things happened on earth as they did in heaven because there was no distinction between the two. God ran the show and people joined him in this good creation. This is the right-side-up ordering of the world.

However, things did not stay this way forever, as we shall soon see . . .

⊛ Do you see the world as a place that was made good and is being redeemed? Why or why not?

⊛ If God is the center of the biblical story, what part do we play?

Day 2

Act 2: Conflict (The Fall)

GENESIS 3:6-7

The woman *approached the tree*, eyed its fruit, and coveted its *mouth-watering, wisdom-granting* beauty. She plucked a fruit from the tree and ate. She then offered *the fruit* to her husband who was close by, and he ate as well. Suddenly their eyes were opened *to a reality previously unknown*. For the first time, they sensed *their vulnerability and rushed to hide* their naked bodies, stitching fig leaves into crude loincloths.

Read the scripture for today and consider:

What do you think it means when the text says, "Suddenly their eyes were opened"?

When God created the good world, sin and death were not part of it. They are foreign, alien entities that have corrupted what God made good and there is nothing "natural" about either of them.

Human beings are responsible for bringing this poison into the world, and we pay for it with our lives. This is the central conflict of the biblical narrative. How will the main character (God) deal with the reality of sin and death in his creation? Everything that was right-side-up is now upside-down and the question is: Will God let this stand or not? This is the true God of the universe, is he not? Will this God get what he always intended: a partnership with his human image bearers? We shall see . . .

※ What does it mean to partner with God today?

※ Do you think God really does get what God wants in the end?

※ Day 3
Act 3: Covenant

GENESIS 12:1–4A, 15:3–6

One day, the Eternal One called out to Abram.

Eternal One: *Abram*, get up and go! Leave your country. Leave your relatives and your father's home, and travel to the land I will show you. *Don't worry—I will guide you there.* I have plans to make a great people from your descendants. And I am going to put a *special* blessing on you and cause your reputation to grow so that you will become a blessing *and example to others.* I will also bless those who bless you *and further you in your journey,* and I'll trip up those who try to trip you *along the way. Through your descendants,* all of the families of the earth will find their blessing in you.

Without any hesitation, Abram went. He did exactly as the Eternal One asked him to do.

[**Abram:**] Since You have not given me the gift of children, my only heir will be one *of the servants* born in my household.

Immediately the word of the Eternal One came to him.

Eternal One: *No, Abram,* this man will not be your heir. No one but your very own child will be an heir for you.

God took him outside *to show him something.*

Eternal One: Look up at the stars, and try to count them all if you can. *There are too many to count!* Your descendants will be *as many* as the stars.

Abram believed God *and trusted in His promises,* so God counted it to his favor as righteousness.

Read the scripture for today and consider:

⊛ What is a covenant?

⊛ What is the promise God made to Abram? Why did God make this promise?

The remarkable thing about the biblical story is that God never gave up on the creation project. After the human beings rebelled and brought sin and death into the world, God did not throw his hands up in the air and quit. Instead, he mounted a rescue mission. In this passage, God began to reveal his plan to Abram.

God promised him that he would be made a great nation and that nation would be blessed in order to be blessing. What God was promising here, in essence, is that through Abram's new family, he would put everything that was broken back together. God is going to heal the world—but he won't do it alone. Instead, God will partner with people to get the job done because that is the way it's supposed to be.

When this covenant was made between Abram—whom God renamed Abraham—and God, something radical happened. God swore to fulfill his end of the promise no matter what Abraham did. In fact, God swore to take any consequence for the breaking of this covenant upon himself. This is the radical and resolute nature of love of the God who created everything. This God gets what he wants, which is to make all things new.

▨ Is it fair for God to swear by himself that the promise to Abram will be kept?

▨ After these three days of meditations how would you answer the question, "What is the gospel?"

 Day 4
Act 4: Climax
Act 5: Church

JOHN 19:30, 20: 21-23

When Jesus drank, He spoke:

Jesus: It is finished!

In that moment, His head fell; and He gave up the spirit.

Jesus: I give you the gift of peace. In the same way the Father sent Me, I am now sending you.

Now He drew close enough to each of them that *they could feel His breath.* He breathed on them:

Jesus: Welcome the Holy Spirit of the living God. You now have the mantle of God's forgiveness. As you go, you are able to share the life-giving power to forgive sins, or to withhold forgiveness.

REVELATION 21:1-5A

I looked again *and could hardly believe my eyes.* Everything above me was new. Everything below me was new. *Everything around me was new* because the heaven and earth that had been passed away, and the sea was gone, completely. And I saw the holy city, the new Jerusalem, descending out of heaven from God, prepared like a bride *on her wedding day,* adorned for her husband *and for His eyes only.* And I heard a great voice, coming from the throne.

A Voice: See, the home of God is with *His* people.
He will live among them;
They will be His people,
And God Himself will be with them.
The prophecies are fulfilled:
He will wipe away every tear from their eyes.
Death will be no more;
Mourning no more, crying no more, pain no more,
For the first things have gone away.

And the One who sat on the throne announced *to His creation,*
The One: See, I am making all things new.

Read the scripture for today and consider:

⬚ What is a covenant?

⬚ What is the promise God makes to Abram? Why does God make this promise?

These three scriptures are like the splashes a stone would make if it were skipped across the lake of the New Testament. They each offer a signpost pointing toward how the big story of the Bible reaches its climax . . . and what happens after that.

When Jesus died on the cross, sin and death were defeated. Fully. Completely. Jesus is the ultimate expression of what divine/

human partnership looks like (because he was fully man and fully God), and his sacrifice marked the end of the upside-down world of the fall. On the cross, it was finished.

What happened next was remarkable.

Jesus was bodily resurrected. This was a foretaste of what is in store for all of us. It is a reminder that God's new world is not simply somewhere else for us to go to after we die but that it is emerging right here, right now. After Jesus rose from the dead, he surprised everyone again when he left the earth. He ascended into heaven and left the Holy Spirit with his disciples. This is the Spirit of God that indwells and empowers Jesus' followers to implement what he accomplished on the cross. The divine/human partnership is back in effect and in Revelation 21 we see where it is all going.

Here we have the vision and promise of the new heaven and a new earth. The dwelling of God is once again with human beings and as it was in the beginning and is now, it also evermore shall be. God will fully and finally make everything new.

⊠ Survey the last four day's readings and meditations. Is this the way you would tell the story of the Bible? Why or why not?

⊠ What readings would you include? Which would you leave out?

INCITING INCIDENT

INTRODUCTION

Every story has a moment when the protagonist is spun right around and catapulted into the series of events and decisions that make up the content of the narrative. In screenwriting circles, this event is called an inciting incident. In the daily readings last week we called it the "conflict" in the story, but this is the event that sends the characters off in a new direction. It changes things, and there is no story without one.

The Bible is full of inciting incidents, and the story of David is no exception. From his anointing at the hands of Samuel to his battle with Goliath and beyond, David's life was shaped by events outside his control that set him on a course to be the king God called him to be. For good or for ill, these occurrences made him who he was and, as such, they became part of his identity.

The same is true of us as well.

All the things that happen to you, be they good or bad, make up your inciting incidents. When you see your life as a story it helps to make sense of what these events were and how they catapulted you into being who you are today. You will hear the inciting incidents of some of the presenters in the video. Their stories are authentic and powerful, but the real question is: What's yours? What are the inciting incidents of your life? What events have most profoundly shaped your motivations and relationships with God, yourself, and others? As Ben says early in the video, "There is no story without an inciting incident." What events drive the story of your life?

CHECKING IN

Last week the "Experiments in Story" section invited you to retell the entire biblical narrative in ten minutes. Share with the group:

▨ Was this experiment easy or difficult?

▨ Why did you choose the story points that you did?

▨ Did you learn anything new about the biblical story as a result of this exercise?

STUDYING THE STORY

THE LIFE OF DAVID, PART 6

Read **1 Samuel 17** (The story of David and Goliath) out loud to the group.

⊛ Do you think this is *the* inciting incident of David's life? Why or why not?

After you have discussed this question, read **1 Chronicles 22:6–10.**

⊛ Does this change your perspective on the David and Goliath story?

⊛ What commentary does this text make regarding the inciting incidents of David's life?

WATCH THE DVD

Watch *Session 6: Inciting Incident.* When the DVD ends, give every-one a moment to reflect and jot down one or two things that they learned, disagreed with, or found surprising.

GROUP DISCUSSION

There are fewer questions this week to leave more time for story-telling. Take this opportunity to practice telling your story.

First Impressions

Before everyone shares in the large group, turn to one or two peo-ple next to you and finish this sentence, "After watching the video about *Inciting Incident* one question I have is . . ."

Community Reflections

1. Pick a favorite novel, film, or play. What is the inciting incident that changes the direction of the story's protagonist?

2. Ben suggests that there is a difference between an inciting inci-dent and tragedy. What do you think he means?

3. What do you think is the inciting incident of the biblical narrative?

4. Chris tells a story about his grandfather and his new car and suggests that the real inciting incidents of our lives are the places where we encounter real love. Do you agree with this?

5. Have you ever had or heard about an experience where someone was changed by love? If so, please share.

6. What would you name as an inciting incident in your life? What would be a helpful way to share this part of the story of your life with others?

EXPERIMENTS IN STORY

Len closed the video with a story about his inciting incident with God. What did you think of his story? What would you name as one of your inciting incidents with God?

Take time today and write down an inciting incident with God. Try to craft it in a way that tells your story.

Bring it to group next week. You will have a chance to share if you would like to.

EXPLORING THE STORY FURTHER

The Bible is one big story full of smaller stories, each with their own inciting incidents. For "Exploring the Story Further" this week we will look at four famous characters from biblical history. Your invitation will be to recall their story as best you can remember and then, using the readings given, imagine what their inciting incident may have been. There is no meditation this week beyond the biblical text. The readings each day are long, so use a Bible you can understand easily.

Day 1

Read **Esther 1 & 2**

Read the scripture for today and consider:

To the best of your memory, what happens after the reading for today?

Now reread this section from the same passage:

ESTHER 2:1-4

A little while later, when King Ahasuerus was no longer angry, he began thinking about Vashti, her actions *that night at the party,* and his decision to dismiss her *from his presence. Seeing the king's mood,* his servants had a suggestion.

Servants: *King Ahasuerus,* someone should find beautiful young women *who are old enough to be married* for you. We suggest you appoint officers in every province of Persia to round up every eligible woman and add her to your harem in the citadel of Susa. Hegai, the king's eunuch who is in charge of the harem, will see to it that all of the women are properly prepared and receive all the needed cosmetics. Then whichever young woman delights you the most will reign as queen in Vashti's place.

King Ahasuerus liked the advice *of his servants* and *gave them permission to* execute the plan.

⊛ Did Esther have any control over the events described above and how they would shape her life?

⊛ Do you think this is her inciting incident? Why or why not?

How do you see the story of Esther fitting in with the whole story of the Bible?

Day 2
Jonah

If you were to retell the story of Jonah in four main bullet-points, what would they be?

Read the book of **Jonah (Chapters 1–4).**

Read the scripture for today and consider:

❋ Did you see anything in this story that you hadn't seen before?

❋ What do you think was Jonah's inciting incident?

Reread **Jonah 1:1–3.**

One day the word of the Eternal One came to *the prophet* Jonah (Amittai's son).

Eternal One: Get up, and go to that powerful *and notorious* city of Nineveh. Call out *My message* against it because the wickedness of its people has come to My attention.

In hearing those instructions, Jonah got up and ran toward Tarshish from the Eternal's presence. He went down to *the port at* Joppa and found a ship bound for Tarshish. He *climbed aboard,* paid the fare, and made himself *comfortable* in the hold of the ship.

❋ Do you see this as Jonah's inciting incident?

How do you see the story of Jonah fitting in with the whole story of the Bible?

Day 3
Mary Magdalene

Reflect on the following questions:

Who was Mary Magdalene?

What do you know about her?

Why is she a famous biblical character?

Now read the following passage from Luke as well as the others listed:

LUKE 8:1–3

Soon after this incident, Jesus preached from city to city, village to village, carry ing the good news of the kingdom of God. He was accompanied by a group called "the twelve," and also by a larger group including some women who had been rescued from evil spirits and healed of diseases. There was Mary, called Magdalene, who had been released from seven demons. There were others like Susanna and Joanna, who was married to Chuza, a steward of King Herod. And there were many others too. *These women played an important role in Jesus' ministry,* using their wealth to provide for Him and His other companions.

Read **Matthew 27: 57–61, John 19:25–26, John 20:1–18.**

❖ What do you think is Mary's inciting incident?

❖ How does her story fit in with the whole narrative of the Bible?

Day 4
The Apostle Paul

Reflect on the following questions:

⊛ Who was Paul?

⊛ What do you know about him?

⊛ What do you think was his inciting incident?

Read **Acts 7:54—8:3** and **Acts 9:1—31.**

⊛ After reading the passages, what do you think is Paul's inciting incident?

How does his name change fit into his inciting incident?

How does his story fit in with the whole narrative of the Bible?

AUTHENTICITY

INTRODUCTION

Have you ever watched a movie and felt like the conflict was resolved a little "too conveniently"? Or, have you ever grumbled that a story's "happy ending" felt forced or that, "things would never work out like that in *real* life"? If so, then you already recognize the power of authenticity in storytelling.

Authenticity, at its roots, is about telling the truth. Stories that seem overly sentimental or emotionally shallow chafe us at a deep level because we know real life is not like that. Real life is messy and complicated and does not always resolve tidily in the end. So, when a storyteller opts to gloss over or avoid the complexity of reality we don't buy it—and we shouldn't, because it is not authentic.

This same thing applies to the way we tell our stories. If the version of events we put forth is always "great" and includes no conflict, struggle, or brokenness, then people will not believe us either. By casting ourselves in this light we are lying, not just about who we really are, but also what our God is like. Part of what Jesus came to do is rescue us from our brokenness and heal us, but this is an ongoing process. If we claim to have no brokenness or need, then we also have no need for rescue.

This is why our last session will explore the value and power of authenticity. What conditions need to be present in order for you to tell the truth? Is it easy or hard for you to be "real" about the light and dark sides of your life? What is the benefit of such honesty anyway? These are the questions you are invited to contemplate and be authentic about during this session.

Author, speaker, and activist Shane Claiborne said that people don't want a church that is sinless. They want a church that is honest.[1] This is a great reminder that we have permission to be honest about our stories. We can own all the good and all the bad, knowing that such honesty will only put us in love's way and open our hearts to experience the grace and love of God.

CHECKING IN

Last week the "Experiments in Story" section invited you to name one of the inciting incidents in your relationship with God.

Take turns and invite everyone to share their inciting incident and then reflect on the following questions:

❈ What is one thing I learned about myself during this experience?

---

1 Shane Claiborne at the Children, Youth, and a New Kind of Christianity conference. Washington, DC. May 2012.

▨ What is one thing I learned about God while exploring his activity in my life?

STUDYING THE STORY
THE LIFE OF DAVID, PART 7

For our last week in "Studying the Story" we are going to reflect on David's words of authenticity from **Psalm 31**.

Read **Psalm 31** out loud twice as a group. Consider:

▨ What kind of life events do you think would precipitate writing a psalm like this?

▨ Have you ever felt the way David does in this psalm? If so, when?

Now, reread **Psalm 31:9–10.**

⊛ How are these verses a picture of true authenticity?

⊛ What can we learn about being truth tellers regarding our need and brokenness from this psalm and the life of David?

WATCH THE DVD

Watch *Session 7: Authenticity.* When the DVD ends, give everyone a moment to reflect and jot down one or two things that they learned, disagreed with, or found surprising.

GROUP DISCUSSION

First Impressions

Before everyone shares in the large group, turn to one or two people next to you and finish this sentence, "After watching the video about *Authenticity* one question I have is . . ."

Community Reflections

1. Can you think of a popular TV show, film, or novel where the ending disappointed you? If so, which one and why?

2. Ben opens the video by asking why Christian storytelling seems to fall short in comparison to what Hollywood and great novelists are doing. Do you agree? Why or why not?

3. It has been said that the most powerful thing you can say to another human being is, "Me too." What do you think this means? How does it relate to what you heard about in the video?

4. What do you think about Chris's point that the Bible doesn't cover up the brokenness of its characters with a sacred text?

Instead it includes all of it for everyone to see. Does this make you trust the authority of the story more or less?

5. What elements of your Christianity make vulnerability difficult? What parts of it enable it to flourish?

6. Ben says, "Our stories are not believable without the darkness." What does he mean by this? Do you think he's right?

7. How do you embrace and be honest about your brokenness without condoning your sin?

8. What are some practices you have found that cultivate authenticity and honesty?

9. How would *you* answer the question Ben puts to the group, "How does one live a well-storied life?"

10. What is one thing you have learned about yourself over the last seven sessions of this journey?

11. What is one thing you have learned about God over the last seven sessions?

EXPERIMENTS IN STORY

This week's lesson is all about authenticity and telling the truth about the needs and struggles in your own story.

Take your journal or use the space below and write a six-line psalm to God expressing your need. Use Psalm 31 as a guide if you need it. Explore not only your need but how you tell the truth openly about it before God.

After you've finished the psalm, find one person you trust and share it with them. Perhaps that person could be a member of your *Power of Your Story* study group. Taking this risk will not be easy, but it will be rewarding because in God's kingdom, authenticity is freedom.

EXPLORING THE STORY FURTHER

Psalm 51 is a powerful psalm because of the author's authenticity. In the psalm, David is brutally honest about himself, his sin, and also his desire to make things right with God. For this final section of "Exploring the Story Further" we will delve into Psalm 51 to see what we can learn about forgiveness.

 *Day 1*

PSALM 51:1-4

> Look on me with a heart of mercy, O God,
>   according to Your generous love.

According to Your great compassion,
  wipe out *every consequence of* my *shameful* crimes.
Thoroughly wash me, *inside and out,* of all my crooked deeds.
  Cleanse me from my sins.
For I am fully aware of all I have done wrong,
  and my guilt is there, staring me in the face.
It was against You, only You, that I sinned,
    for I have done what You say is wrong, right before Your
      eyes.
So when You speak, You are in the right.
  When You judge, Your judgments are pure and true.

The psalm opens with a heartfelt plea for mercy and grace. However, what is powerful is that David did not try to cover up what he did or skirt responsibility. He says to God, "It was against You, only You, that I sinned, for I have done what You say is wrong, right before Your eyes."

This is not someone offering a half-apology or trying to save his public image. This is the face of true contrition, and this honesty is what opened the door for David's healing. In fact, it is illustrative of the first phase of forgiveness: naming the offense. Whether it is a broken relationship with God or others, the first step toward healing is telling the truth about what has happened.

When you have done wrong, is it difficult to admit it openly? Why or why not?

 Think of a time you were honest like this when you asked for mercy from another person. How did it go? What can you learn from the psalm about this?

Day 2

PSALM 51:5-9

For I was guilty from the day I was born,
    a sinner from the time my mother became pregnant with
        me.
But still, You long *to enthrone* truth throughout my being;
    in unseen places deep within me, You show me wisdom.
Cleanse me *of my wickedness* with hyssop, and I will be clean.
    If You wash me, I will be whiter than snow.
Help me hear joy and happiness *as my accompaniment,*
    so my bones, which You have broken, will *dance in* delight
        instead.
Cover Your face so You will not see my sins,
    and erase my guilt *from the record.*

When a relationship is broken, the first step toward forgiveness involves acknowledging what has transpired between the two parties as openly and honestly as possible. If the offender and the offended are not able to tell the truth, restoration can only go so far. The next step toward forgiveness comes when the offense is disclosed and truly revealed for what it is. This means the transgression between the two parties is not only divulged but it is definitively declared to be wrong.

We see this in Psalm 51:5–9 today. David's sin was before him and he owned up to it. It had been acknowledged. However, it had also been totally disclosed and the pain of this made David uncomfortable. "Hide your face from my sins," he cried out. The shame of our sins can be hard to bear, but shame is not the end.

David also asked to be cleansed, and that cleansing would come. Condemnation is not the end of the story, but before a transgression can be healed, it must be both acknowledged and disclosed.

▨ Disclosing an offense between two parties means saying that what happened is not okay. How do you do this in a way that keeps the door open for reconciliation?

▨ What is the difference between saying, "I forgive you," and saying, "It's okay" to someone who has sinned against you?

Day 3

PSALM 51:10-14

Create in me a clean heart, O God;
  restore within me a sense of being brand new.
Do not throw me far away from Your presence,
  and do not remove Your Holy Spirit from me.
Give back to me the *deep* delight of being saved by You;
  let Your willing Spirit sustain me.
If You do, I promise to teach rebels Your ways
  and help sinners find their way back to You.
Free me from the guilt *of murder,* of shedding *a man's* blood,
  O God who saves me.
    Now my tongue, *which was used to destroy,* will be used to
      sing with deep delight of how right *and just* You are.

As if the first two parts of forgiveness (acknowledging and disclosing the offense) were not hard enough, the next step might be the most difficult. In the third phase of forgiveness the offended tells the truth about what has happened, names the person responsible, and then releases the offender from the debt of the offense. The sinner is set free by the one who has been sinned against. This is forgiveness, and we see how David asked for it in Psalm 51 today.

David asked to have a clean heart created in him. He begged for a right spirit. He pleaded not to be cast out of the Lord's presence.

He was utterly vulnerable and at the mercy of the offended (God, in the context of this psalm), and it was from that place that he asked for mercy. Such vulnerability can be risky and frightening, but it creates the conditions for forgiveness and reconciliation to happen. Nothing else will.

▨ Can you think of a time when you had to be vulnerable before someone you sinned against? How did it go?

▨ What can you learn about forgiving others who are in your debt from that memory and from the psalm today?

▨ What can you learn about receiving forgiveness from that memory and from the psalm today?

 *Day 4*

PSALM 51:15-19

O Lord, *pry* open my lips
     that this mouth will sing *joyfully* of Your greatness.
I would surrender *my dearest possessions or destroy all that I*
          prize to prove my regret,
     but You don't take pleasure in sacrifices or burnt offerings.
What sacrifice I can offer You is my broken spirit
     because a broken spirit, O God,
     a heart that honestly regrets the past,
You won't detest.
Be good to Zion; grant her Your favor.
     Make Jerusalem's walls steady and strong.
Then there will be sacrifices made,
     burnt offerings and whole burnt offerings,
With right motives that will delight You.
     And *costly* young bulls will be offered up to Your altar, *for*
          only the best.

For the last three days we have explored the phases required in order for healthy forgiveness to take place. First, the offense between the two parties must be acknowledged. Second, it must be then disclosed and declared to be "not okay." The third and final step comes when the offended person releases the offender from any debt, with no strings attached. One of the things that can cloud this process is when the offender wants to "work off" the debt to the offended. Phrases like, "I'll make it up to you," or "Let me pay you back," are not a part of forgiveness, because forgiveness is a gift. It cannot be earned or else it is not forgiveness.

In the final section of Psalm 51 we see that David understood this. He declared that it was not sacrifice but instead a broken heart and humble spirit that would bring delight to God. David realized he could not earn God's forgiveness with good religion. Only a broken heart would do, and that David had in spades.

- When you have wronged someone else have you ever felt tempted to try and "work it off"? Why or why not?

- Have you ever had someone try to "make it up" to you? What was the result?

- Do you agree that you cannot earn forgiveness because it is a gift? Why or why not?

We pray that over the past several weeks you and your group have encountered the truth of God's story in new ways, and that your lives will be forever changed as a result. We pray that as you close this study, you will go out with the knowledge that God can and will work powerfully through your story.

GINNY OWENS

BEN ARMENT

CHRIS SEAY

LEONARD SWEET

PETE WILSON

ABOUT THE AUTHORS

Ben Arment has launched a variety of creative projects, including STORY and Dream Year. He serves as a development strategist for several national organizations and wrote the book *Church in the Making* through B&H Publishing. Ben and his wife, Ainsley, live in Virginia Beach, Virginia with their three boys, Wyatt, Dylan, and Cody. You can find him at BenArment.com and Twitter at @BenArment.

Ginny Owens is a three-time Dove Award winner and the Gospel Music Association's 2000 New Artist of the Year recipient. She has sold nearly one million albums and has been a top performer on the Christian radio charts with hits like "If You Want Me To," "Free," and "I Wanna Be Moved." When not touring, Owens serves as an adjunct professor of songwriting at Belmont University and as one of the worship leaders at The People's Church in Franklin, Tennessee.

Chris Seay is a church planter, pastor, president of Ecclesia Bible Society, and internationally acclaimed speaker. His six books include *The Gospel According to Lost, The Gospel According to Tony Soprano,* and *Faith of My Fathers.*

Leonard Sweet is the E. Stanley Jones Professor of Evangelism at Drew University (New Jersey), a distinguished visiting professor at George Fox University (Oregon), and a weekly contributor to Sermons.com and the podcast *Napkin Scribbles.* A pioneer in online learning with some of the highest "influence" rankings of any religious figure in the world of social media (Twitter,

Facebook), he has authored numerous articles, sermons, and more than fifty books.

Pete Wilson is the founding and senior pastor of Cross Point Church in Nashville, Tennessee. Pete desires to see churches become radically devoted to Christ, irrevocably committed to one another, and relentlessly dedicated to reaching those outside of God's family. Pete and his wife, Brandi, have three boys and live in Nashville, Tennessee. Pete is an avid blogger (www.PeteWilson .tv) and enjoys hunting, gardening, and watching football when he's not preaching.